Portraits in GRACE

A CANTATA FOR HOLY WEEK

By Joseph M. Martin • Orchestration by Brad Nix

① This symbol indicates a track number on the StudioTrax CD (accompaniment only) or SplitTrax CD

Performance Time ca. 45 minutes

ISBN 9-781-5400-0671-4

SHAWNEE PRESS

EXCLUSIVELY DISTRIBUTED BY

HAL•LEONARD®

7777 W. BLUEMOUND RD. P.O. BOX 13819 MILWAUKEE, WI 53213

In Australia Contact:
Hal Leonard Australia Pty. Ltd.
4 Lentara Court
Cheltenham, Victoria, 3192 Australia
Email: ausadmin@halleonard.com.au

Visit Hal Leonard Online at
www.halleonard.com/church
Visit Shawnee Press Online at
www.shawneepress.com

FOREWORD

Creation displays the wonder and beauty of God in a thousand miraculous ways. With each golden sunrise, God renews the shining promises of life within us. In the noonday, He decorates our journey of faith with the magnificent colors of peace and joy. In the evening, each sparkling star splashes silver promise upon the canvases of our souls.

How great is our God, the Creator! How marvelous is the art of His hands! Like a gallery of grace, God's eternal truth is gifted to us in vivid hues of hope and assurance.

In the brilliance of the universe, we glimpse the glory of God. Yet this glory pales in comparison to the radiant splendor of Jesus. In Him, we see the true colors of divine love and grace. Nothing can compare with the surpassing beauty of knowing Him.

Today, as we gather to consider His remarkable life, may our vision be renewed and, as we worship, may we clearly see God's perfect portrait of grace.

PERFORMANCE NOTES

Throughout the cantata, I have attempted to join musical works with visual images to support the message of the texts. Each movement can be visually represented by a work of art created by members of your congregation, by sculptures and icons, or by images available for projection from public domain Internet sources. If banners or tapestries are used, an important word or phrase may represent the focus of each anthem.

PRELUDE: During the PRELUDE, slowly bring in eight works of art ("portraits"), each representing the various movements of the cantata. Place them across the front of the worship space. As each movement is sung and completed, drape a black cloth over or around the respective piece of art. If candles are used for illumination, these elements can also be extinguished to further heighten the sense of drama. As the work progresses, the shadows created by this action reflect the deep sorrow of Christ's suffering.

PORTRAIT: This anthem delivers images representing the many ways we see Christ reflected in creation.
   Images: sunrise, mountain scenery, a starry sky, a rose
   Objects: a long stem rose
   Words: Creator

FAIREST LORD JESUS: A time-honored text that speaks to the layers of beauty, both natural and spiritual, found in Christ's divine character.
   Images: gentle nature scenes, Jesus as the Good Shepherd, Jesus with children
   Objects: a shepherd's crook
   Words: Savior

THE HEALER: This anthem offers a portrait of Christ, the Great Physician.
  Images: the hands of Christ, Christ working miracles among the people
  Objects: anointing oil, a basin and towel
  Words: Healer, Miracle

BEHOLD THE KING: This dramatic anthem describes the triumphal entry of Jesus into Jerusalem.
  Images: palms, Christ entering Jerusalem
  Objects: a vase of palm fronds
  Words: King, Hosanna

WE REMEMBER: This is a tableau of the upper room and Christ's last supper.
  Images: the last supper
  Objects: bread and chalice
  Words: Remember, Mercy

THE SACRED GARDEN: This anthem takes the listener to the garden of Gethsemane.
  Images: Christ praying in the garden, praying hands, olive branch
  Objects: A white candle (representing the comforting angel) and a red candle (representing Jesus). Other multi-colored candles set apart from the angel and the Christ candle can represent the sleeping disciples.
  Words: Betrayal, Surrender, Prayer

LET US GATHER IN THE SHADOW OF THE CROSS: This expressive anthem moves us to Calvary and the images of the crucifixion begin to be displayed.
  Images: classic cross images, crown of thorns
  Objects: a cross, a crown of thorns, large nails
  Words: Lamb of God, Redeemer

PORTRAIT OF THE CROSS / RECESSIONAL: This final anthem carries us to Christ's death and the deep sorrow of His final act of grace and love.
  Images: the crucified Christ, Jesus being taken from the cross, Pieta (Mary holding the slain Jesus)
  Objects: A large candle that is extinguished during the final instrumental postlude. The candle can be carried slowly down the center aisle and out into the night to represent Christ's body being taken to the garden tomb. The service ends in shadows as the candles are extinguished and the rest of the altar and the front of the sanctuary are draped in black. The final postlude can be repeated to allow a silent departure from the church building.

Please feel free to use your own ideas and to adapt these suggestions to fit your own rituals and traditions.

PRELUDE

Tune:
CRUSADERS' HYMN
Schlesische Volkslieder, 1842
Arranged by
JOSEPH M. MARTIN (BMI)

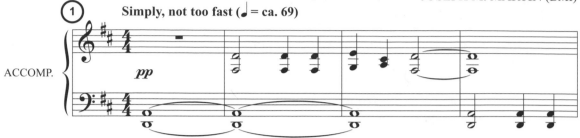

NARRATION 1

The Beauty of Jesus, the Creator.

Creation displays the wonder and beauty of God in a thousand miraculous ways. With each golden sunrise, God renews the shining promises of life within us. In the noonday, He decorates our journey of faith with the magnificent colors of peace and joy. In the evening, each sparkling star splashes silver promise upon the canvases of our souls.

How great is our God, the Creator! How marvelous is the art of His hands! Like a gallery of grace, God's eternal truth is gifted to us in vivid hues of hope and assurance.

In the brilliance of the universe, we glimpse the glory of God. Yet this glory pales in comparison to the radiant splendor of Jesus. In Him, we see the true colors of divine love and grace. Nothing can compare with the surpassing beauty of knowing Him.

Today, as we gather to consider His remarkable life, may our vision be renewed and, as we worship, may we clearly see God's perfect portrait of grace.

Hear this word from Scripture:*

The Word became flesh and made His dwelling among us. We have seen His glory, the glory of the one and only Son, who came from the Father, full of grace and truth. *(John 1:14)*

PORTRAIT

Words by
JOSEPH MARY PLUNKETT (1887-1916), *alt.*

Music by
DIANE HANNIBAL (ASCAP)
Arranged by
JOSEPH M. MARTIN (BMI)

PORTRAITS IN GRACE - SATB

eyes. His bod-y gleams a-mid the win-ter snows. His

tears fall from the skies.

TENOR

BASS

God of won - ders. God of mar - vel and
God of won - ders. God of light.

mys - ter - y. God of won-ders. God of won-ders.
God of won - ders. God of won - ders.

Each wind-ing

12

path   by   sa - cred   feet   are   worn.   His   lov - ing

heart   stirs   the   ev - er - beat - ing   sea.

His crown is   twined   with   our

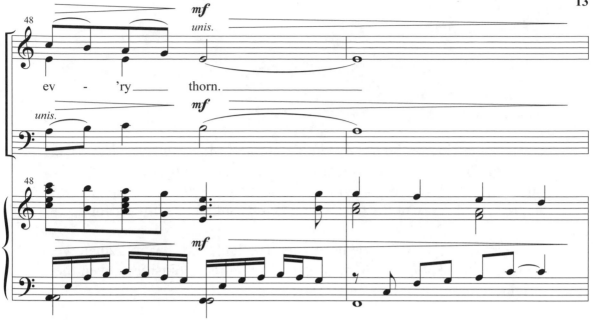

NARRATION 2

The Beauty of Jesus, the Savior.

Jesus is the Lily of the Valley, the Bright and Morning Star. He is the Rose of Sharon and the fairest of ten thousand. No poet's rhyme is sufficient to describe His glory. No painter's brush can adequately express the beauty of the One who loved us and gave Himself for us.

Though, in His earthly appearance, He had "no beauty…that we should desire Him," the perfection of His holiness outshines even the brightest and best of heaven's angels.

commissioned in celebration of the 25th anniversary of
Reverend Rebecca Migliore's pastorate to the Presbyterian churches of West Orange, NJ

FAIREST LORD JESUS

Words:
(st. 1-3) Anonymous
(st. 4) JOSEPH AUGUSTUS SEISS (1823-1904)

Incorporating tunes:
BUNESSAN
Traditional Gaelic Melody
and **CRUSADERS' HYMN**
Schlesische Volkslieder, 1842
Arranged by
JOSEPH M. MARTIN (BMI)

ture, O Thou of God and man,___ the

Son;_____ Thee will I cher - ish.

Thee will I hon - or, Thou my soul's glo -

ry, joy,___ and crown.

(end solo)

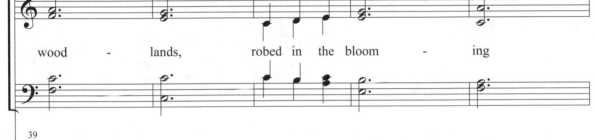

cresc. poco a poco

er.   Je - sus   is   pur - er.   Je - sus makes

wound - ed   hearts   to sing.

Ah

20

Je - sus shines pur - er than all the an - gels heav'n can boast.

Tempo I (♩ = ca. 124)

NARRATION 3

The Beauty of Jesus, the Healer.

The gospel of Matthew tells us that "Jesus went through all the towns and villages, teaching in their synagogues, proclaiming the good news of the kingdom, and healing every disease and sickness."

Jesus was moved by compassion for those in need. In His graceful touch, we see with perfect clarity His service to body, mind and spirit. Through His ministry and humility, Christ, the Great Physician, fulfilled the Scripture: "Surely He took up our pain and bore our suffering…and by His wounds we are healed."

THE HEALER

Words by
WILLIAM HUNTER (1811-1877)

Music by
JOSEPH M. MARTIN (BMI)
Incorporating tune:
GREAT PHYSICIAN
by JOHN H. STOCKTON (1813-1877)

speaks the wound - ed heart to cheer. Oh, ___

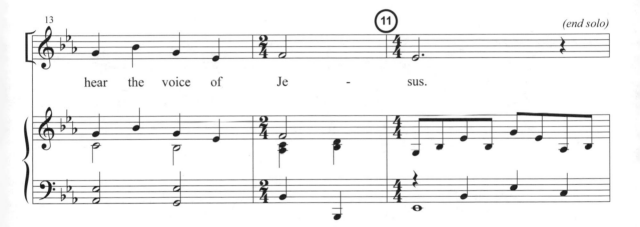

hear the voice of Je - sus.

(end solo)

SOPRANO

ALTO

Your ___ man - y sins ___ are ___ all for -

TENOR

BASS

giv'n. Oh,___ hear the voice of Je -

sus.___ Go___ on your way in peace to

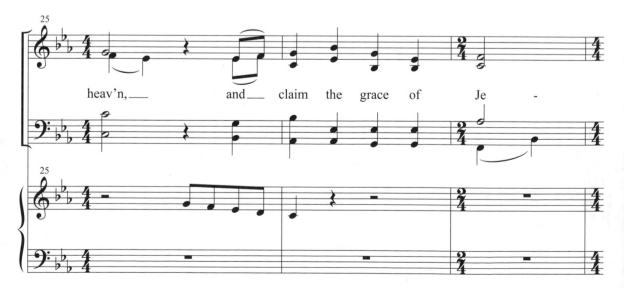

heav'n,___ and___ claim the grace of Je -

28

NARRATION 4

The Beauty of Jesus, the King.

Jesus' work was a steady procession of promise. As He travelled throughout the land, His teaching and acts of healing endeared Him to the people. His miracles of mercy and grace led many to proclaim Him the long-awaited Messiah. As His fame continued to grow, so too did the people's hope that He was the rightful heir to David's throne. Wherever He went, large groups of people followed Him.

As Jesus entered the ancient city of Jerusalem, the crowds surged and a parade of palms began to move through the city. The people started to shout, "Hosanna to the Son of David! Blessed is He who comes in the name of the Lord!" The whole gathering of disciples began to rejoice and praise God with a loud voice for all the mighty works they had seen. For just a moment it seemed as though the entire world was following Him.

BEHOLD THE KING

Words and Music by
JOSEPH M. MARTIN (BMI)

38

far be - yond the pal - ace walls.

far be - yond the pal - ace walls.

All earth - ly ti - tles He de -

nies; to claim an e - ven high - er

crown of thorns, ___ a scar - let robe, a

lone - ly cross His on - ly throne. Be -

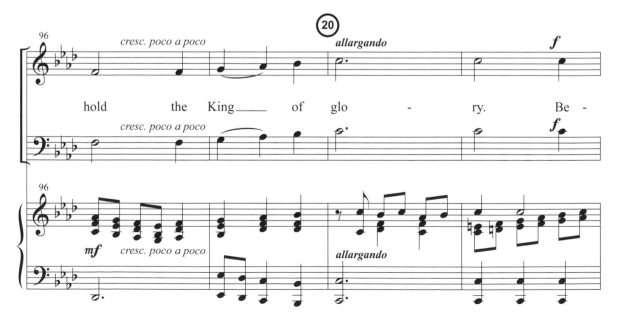

cresc. poco a poco **allargando** *f*

hold the King ___ of glo - ry. Be -

hold   the   King   of   glo -   ry.

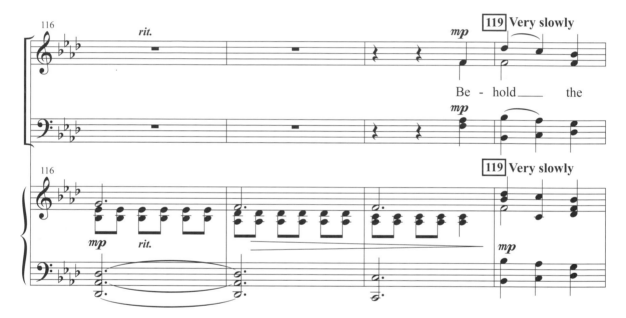

Be - hold   the

King   of   glo -   ry.

NARRATION 5

The Beauty of Jesus, the Passover Lamb.

After His triumphant entry into Jerusalem, Jesus continued to teach and call the people to faith. As the time approached for the traditional Hebrew commemoration of Passover, He gathered with His disciples in a cloistered upper room. There, He revealed to them the deeper truths of His mission of redemption. In this poignant setting, Christ shared a new covenant with His chosen ones, a sacred bond established in divine love and mercy. As we pause to reflect on the beauty of this scene, let us remember that in the simple elements of bread and wine, God created a portrait of grace.

WE REMEMBER

Words by
JOSEPH M. MARTIN (BMI)

Music by
JOSEPH M. MARTIN
and MICHAEL E. SHOWALTER (ASCAP)

mem - ber. In the bread and in the wine, we can

know Your love di - vine. It's the sea - son, it's the time, to re-

poco rit.

a tempo

mem - ber.

TENOR

BASS

As we

bow our heads in prayer, we re - mem - ber. In the

fel - low - ship we share, we re - mem - ber. In the

still - ness of this space, we are safe in love's em - brace. Let us

48

Great I Am,____ we will re-mem - ber You.

In the

mys - t'ry of this feast, we re-mem - ber. As we

50

52

NARRATION 6

The Beauty of Jesus, the Man of Sorrows.

That same evening, Jesus took three of His disciples with Him to a walled garden where He often prayed. There, underneath a canopy of olive trees, He confronted the deep shadows that gathered near. He prayed to His Father for relief but surrendered to the greater purpose that had sent Him to earth. Kneeling in the quiet solitude of Gethsemane, Jesus faced His destiny and chose the path of grace.

A SACRED GARDEN

Words and Music by
JOSEPH M. MARTIN (BMI)
Incorporating tune:
STAR OF THE COUNTY DOWN
Traditional Irish Melody

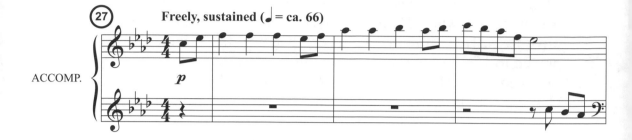

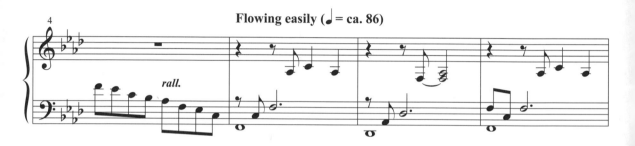

gen - tle,__ qui - et__ place, with a chap - el made of__

star - light 'neath the can - o - py of space; and

there the Sav - ior__ paus - es be - neath the__ an - cient__

trees. He looks in-to the sol - emn sky, and

falls up - on His knees.

Fa - ther, Fa - ther, Thy will be

done.

There is a sacred garden, above the cities glare, where the scent of fragrant roses rises like a

prayer.___ 'Tis there a - mid the__ beau - ty, Christ__

leans up - on a__ stone. Sur - round - ed__ by the__

shad - dows, He__ prays and__ weeps a - lone.

60

there the Lamb of Sor - rows will find a rest - ing place; and in that sa - cred gar - den, will change the world with grace. Fa - ther, will

Fa - ther, Thy will be done.

Fa - ther, Fa - ther, Thy will be

Grandly (♩ = ca. 56)

done! Thy will be done!

NARRATION 7

The Beauty of Jesus, the Redeemer.

Jesus was delivered to Pilate's court where He was interrogated. Bowing to pressure from the religious leaders of the day, Pilate handed Him over to be beaten and crucified. Centurions placed a purple robe on His back and a twisted crown of thorns upon His head. Kneeling before Him, they mocked Him, calling out, "Hail, king of the Jews!" Then they led Him to a place called "Golgotha," where they crucified Him along with two common criminals.

As the sun arched across the darkened sky, the cross began to cast a shadow of redemption across the land. As Jesus uttered His parting words from the cross, He spoke forgiveness and mercy into eternity. Upon that windswept hill, He reached out with open arms to a world lost in sin and sorrow. With one last gesture of eternal love, Jesus gathered His children close to His heart.

for Bruce Bush

LET US GATHER IN THE SHADOW OF THE CROSS

Words by
JOSEPH M. MARTIN (BMI)

Music by
BRAD NIX (ASCAP)

qui - et, sol-emn place, may we   learn the cost of   grace.   Let us

find our place on Cal - va - ry.   Ky - ri - e   e -

TENOR

BASS

le - i - son,   ky - ri - e   e - le - i - son.

cross.   Let   us   think up - on   the   stream.   In   His

think up - on   His   crim - son   flow - ing   stream._____   In   His

cross.   Let   us   think up - on   the   stream.   In   His

think up - on   His   crim - son   flow - ing   stream._____   In   His

cresc.

death,   our   lives   are   sealed,   with   His   wounds,   our   hearts   are

cresc.

death,   our   lives   are   sealed,   with   His   wounds,   with   His

cresc.

death,   our   lives   are   sealed,   with   His   wounds,   our   hearts   are

cresc.

death,   our   lives   are   sealed,   with   His   wounds,   our   hearts   are

cresc.

Kyrie, kyrie eleison.

kyrie, kyrie eleison.

Let us gather in the shadow of the cross.

NARRATION 8

The Beauty of Jesus, the Grace-Giver.

Many years have passed since that terrible day of sorrows. The silhouette of the empty cross has now become a universal portrait of grace for the world. The beauty of this sacred image is beyond compare in the eyes of those who love Jesus. It is the living art of heaven, the crowning glory of Christ's redeeming work.

This is our sacred season of remembrance. This is our time to recall, reflect and repent. As we gaze upon the cross of Christ, let us bring His extraordinary life to our hearts and minds. May we recommit our lives to His grand design and reflect His beauty in our own lives. May we lean willingly into the Potter's hand and submit to be fashioned by His will, trusting that He is faithful to finish the work He has already begun in us. Finish us, Lord Jesus. We surrender all to you!

PORTRAIT OF THE CROSS

Words by
ISAAC WATTS (1674-1748), *alt.*

Music by
JOSEPH M. MARTIN (BMI)

* Tune: PASSION CHORALE, Hans Leo Hassler, 1564-1612

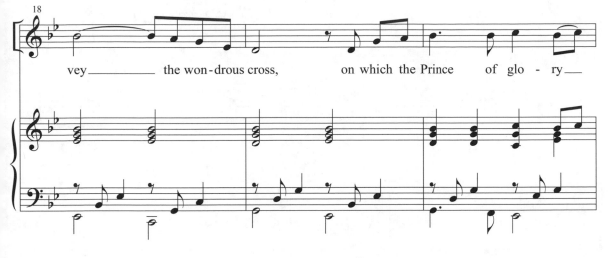

vey_____ the won-drous cross, on which the Prince of glo - ry___

died, my rich-est gain I count but loss, and

pour con-tempt on all my pride._____

(end solo)

sor - row _ meet, or thorns com - pose so rich a crown,

or thorns com - pose so rich a crown,

or thorns com - pose so rich a

or thorns com - pose so rich a crown?

crown, com - pose so rich a crown?

Lamb of God.

It is

It is fin - ished.

fin - shed.   It is   fin - ished.

(end choir)

RECESSIONAL OF SHADOWS

Tune: **PASSION CHORALE**
by HANS LEO HASSLER (1564-1612)
Arranged by
JOSEPH M. MARTIN (BMI)

86